ABSURD ART!

WACKY WORLD OF...

by
Hermione Redshaw

BEARPORT PUBLISHING

Minneapolis, Minnesota

FUSION

CREDITS

All images are courtesy of Shutterstock.com, unless otherwise specified. With thanks to Getty Images, Thinkstock Photo, and iStockphoto.

Recurring assets – Lelene (header font), MaryMB (explosion), RoyaltyFreeStockVectors (spiral), Ardea, hvostik (series logo), Amy Li (additional illustrations). Cover – Ian Knox (wiki commons), Dolfilms, p2–3 – Impact Photography, p4–5 – Fedor Selivanov, Baloncici, Prostock-Studio (iStock), p6–7 – Nasch92 (wiki commons), Roger Higgins (wiki commons), p8–9 – Daderot (wiki commons), Patche99z (wiki commons), p10–11 – TashaNatasha, DragonTiger8, anya_Terekhina, Abdoabdalla, p12–13 – Agent001 (wiki commons), p14–15 – EdgarMueller (wiki commons), Lee Jordan (wiki commons), Mr.Atoz (wiki commons), p16–17 – baldezh, imagewriter, Santiago Marquez, p18–19 – Dominic Robinson (wiki commons), Infrogmation of New Orlean (wiki commons), p20–21 – Zzzenia, Lucy.Brown, TashaNatasha, p22–23 – Biswarup Ganguly (wiki commons), Andrew Russeth (wiki commons), Ank Kumar (wiki commons), Warut Chinsai, Zurijeta.

Library of Congress Cataloging-in-Publication Data is available at www.loc.gov or upon request from the publisher.

ISBN: 979-8-88509-380-4 (hardcover)
ISBN: 979-8-88509-502-0 (paperback)
ISBN: 979-8-88509-617-1 (ebook)

© 2023 Booklife Publishing
This edition is published by arrangement with Booklife Publishing.

North American adaptations © 2023 Bearport Publishing Company. All rights reserved. No part of this publication may be reproduced in whole or in part, stored in any retrieval system, or transmitted in any form or by any means, electronic, mechanical, photocopying, recording, or otherwise, without written permission from the publisher.

For more information, write to Bearport Publishing, 5357 Penn Avenue South, Minneapolis, MN 55419.

CONTENTS

ART 4
LOBSTER TELEPHONE 6
MUD MAID 8
ROCKY ART 10
SHARK TANK 12
CHALK ART 14
ILLUSIONS 16
BANKSY 18
STENCIL ART 20
ALMOST ABSURD 22
GLOSSARY 24
INDEX 24

ART

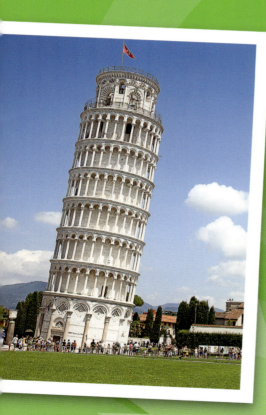

There is no doubt that humans do some very strange things. We build kooky buildings and make umbrellas for pets. Some people are even trying to turn water into gold.

When it comes to art, we've gone from carving in stone to creating magnificent **modern** masterpieces. With wacky artists and even wilder artwork, it's time to question everything you know about the world of art.

LOBSTER TELEPHONE

Ring, ring! In 1938, Salvador Dalí put a lobster on a telephone. Why? He believed that seeing **random** objects together could make people think more deeply about the world around them.

DALÍ WAS A SURREALIST. THIS GROUP OF ARTISTS WAS KNOWN FOR PUTTING ODD OBJECTS TOGETHER.

Salvador Dalí

Dalí made many quirky **sculptures** and strange paintings. He is often thought of as a leading artist of his time.

MUD MAID

What about making art out of nature? Sue and Pete Hill made Mud Maid entirely out of mud, sand, moss, and ivy. This garden growth looks like a giant woman sleeping in the Lost Gardens of Heligan in Cornwall, England.

Mud Maid is a living sculpture. All the plants that grow on her are alive. That means her hair and clothes change with the seasons.

She might be dressed in white when it's snowing in winter. Her outfit changes to reds and browns in autumn when all the leaves fall.

ROCKY ART

The Hills were not the first to use nature in art. Humans have been doing it for many years. The results can be absurd but also amazing!

Stonehenge was made thousands of years ago using huge rocks.

Modern artists sometimes use rocks, too. But they may be much smaller. Some people paint rocks and leave them around outside for others to find.

Grab your own rock and some paint. Then, make your own rocking art!

SHARK TANK

Artist Damien Hirst is best known for making art from dead animals in tanks. His shark art made a splash!

Hirst's shark wasn't popular with everyone. Eddie Saunders had a shark on **display** in his electrical shop before Hirst made the shark art. Saunders later sold it to a **gallery** with the title A Dead Shark Isn't Art.

Whenever people said anyone could have made his art, Hirst responded, "But you didn't, did you?"

CHALK ART

What about art below your feet? Sometimes, you have to look down to find art. Instead of doing art on something they can keep forever, some artists use pavement.

Chalk art can be washed away in a storm. People walk across it and smudge it off the sidewalk.

14

Chalk artists Julian Beever, Edgar Müller, Tracy Lee Stum, and Kurt Wenner create a whole new world with their art. They make **3D** art that tricks you into thinking the ground isn't flat.

15

ILLUSIONS

Like 3D chalk art, illusion art looks or seems different than what is really happening. With this type of art, you often need to be looking at the piece from the right spot for it to work.

Some illusions can be confusing no matter how you look at them. Check out this one, for example. Do you see a vase or two faces?

This art could be either faces or a vase! Some illusions don't really make sense.

BANKSY

The most absurd thing about one British artist is that no one knows who he is. Banksy uses stencils to create art very quickly wherever he goes.

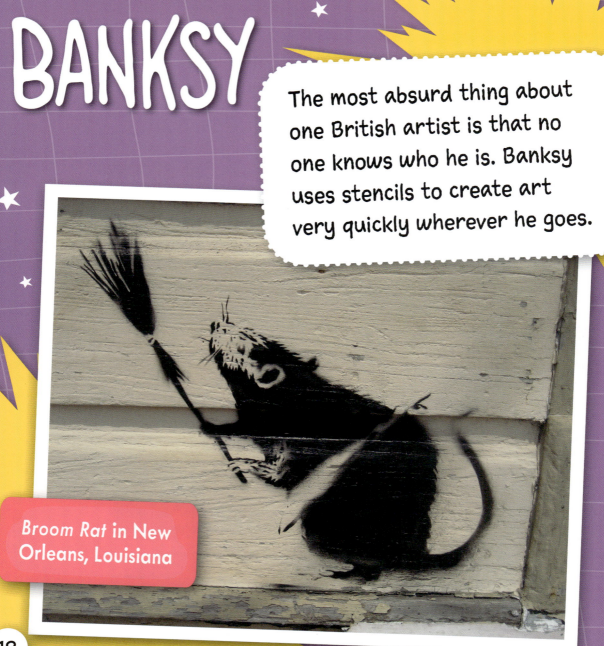

Broom Rat in New Orleans, Louisiana

One of Banksy's most famous artworks is *Girl with Balloon*. In 2018, a painted version of this art suddenly **shredded** itself right after someone bought it! Then, Banksy called the piece by the new name *Love Is in the Bin*.

Banksy was the only one who knew his painting would shred.

STENCIL ART

Stencilling is the opposite of cutting a shape out. You use the shape that's left behind to make art. Try making your own stencil using cardboard.

Banksy used paint for his art, but you can use whatever you want. Color in your shape with paints, pens, pencils . . . or even glitter. Why not try something absurd?!

WHEN YOU TAKE AWAY THE STENCIL, THE COLOR STAYS BEHIND.

ALMOST ABSURD

Check out even more art!

THE ARTIST IS PRESENT
- By Marina Abramović
- Made in 2010
- The artist of this piece sat in a chair in an art museum

MUSEUM OF THE MOON
- By Luke Jerram
- Made in 2016
- A blow-up moon the size of a two-story house

THE ART OF BRICK
- By Nathan Sawaya
- Made in 2007
- A set of sculptures made from plastic bricks

When it comes to art, nothing is ever too absurd. In fact, sometimes the most absurd art can be the best art.

23

GLOSSARY

display out for show

gallery a room or building in which people look at works of art

modern having to do with the present time

random lacking a clear plan, pattern, or purpose

sculptures pieces of art that are made by carving or otherwise shaping materials

shredded cut or torn into long, thin pieces

3D something that is not or does not look flat

INDEX

Banksy 18–19, 21
chalk 14–16
illusion 16–17
nature 8, 10
rocks 10–11
sculpture 7, 9, 22
shark 12–13
stencil 18, 20–21
3D 15–16